A FULL MONTH'S WORTH OF NAGGING

FRIDGE NOTES FROM DAD XO

A FULL MONTH'S WORTH OF NAGGING

FRED BRACE

ONION RIVER PRESS

Burlington, Vermont

Fridge Notes From Dad
(A Full Month's Worth of Nagging)

Copyright © 2024
By Fred Brace

Onion River Press
Burlington, VT 05401
info@onionriverpress.com
www.onionriverpress.com

ISBN: 978-1-957184-75-3
Library of Congress Control Number: 2024919799.

Dear Madilyn & Isabelle —

Unless otherwise noted, these notes were painstakingly handcrafted and then lovingly polished by yours truly with the hope that some of them might come in handy from time-to-time during your life journey.

Heads up !! I hope to discuss these notes with you when the timing is right... So pay attention. There will be pop quizzes from time to time.

Love always & forever,
Dad
XO

Vol I (1-31)

- PERSONAL HYGIENE
- LAUGHTER
- GRUDGES
- EAT YOUR VEGGIES
- GARLIC & OLIVE OIL
- FAMILY FUNCTIONS
- JOB SECURITY
- GREENER PASTURES
- THE TWIST
- POLITICS
- RELIGION
- MONEY
- BIRDS & BEES
- COOKING
- BREAD & CHEESE

WEAKNESSES
TRASH TALK
VOLUNTEER
ANIMAL RESCUE
GRATITUDE THERAPY
LEAD, FOLLOW, OR.
AFFECTION
ANGER MGMT
BRAKE PEDAL
PLAN B
WISDOM
PICKING FLOWERS
BORROWING STUFF
THANK YOU CARDS
OREO® COOKIE
RAISING CHILDREN

PERSONAL HYGIENE

KEEP YOUR NOSE AND
YOUR KARMA CLEAN.

XO
DAD

1/31

LAUGHTER

I'VE READ THAT LAUGHTER
IS A GREAT FORM OF CARDIO
EXERCISE. I'LL BET IT'S
ALSO GREAT CONDITIONING FOR
OUR SPIRIT... LAUGH OFTEN.

DAD

BTW... BELLY LAUGHS COUNT AS
        EXTRA WORKOUT CREDITS.

2/31

GRUDGES

TRY NOT TO CARRY GRUDGES
FOR TOO LONG...
THEY TEND TO BECOME AWFULLY
HEAVY. THEY CAN SUCK UP YOUR
ENERGY AND ROB YOU OF FORWARD
PROGRESS IN YOUR LIFE.
THEY CAN ALSO EAT YOU UP INSIDE,
MAKIN' YOU SICK.

THE ONLY MEDICINE AND TREATMENT
I'VE BEEN ABLE TO FIND IS
FORGIVENESS. LEARN THE LESSON
THE GRUDGE OFFERS, START TO
FORGIVE, THROW THE UGLY GRUDGE
INTO A DITCH ALONGSIDE THE ROAD,
AND THEN BE ON YOUR WAY...

3/31   XO DAD ☮

EAT YOUR VEGGIES

During your TEENS commit
TO BEING A VEGETARIAN FOR
AT LEAST 30-90 DAYS.
You'll END UP LEARNING
A LIFETIME OF HEALTHY
NUTRITION INFO.
You'll ALSO BE DOING YOUR
BODY, THE PLANET AND
CERTAIN ANIMALS A BIG FAVOR.

XO
DAD
BON APPETIT

4/31

Garlic & Olive Oil

A HOUSE WITHOUT FRESH
GARLIC & OLIVE OIL CAN
NEVER TRULY BE A HOME.

XO
DAD

5/31

FAMILY FUNCTIONS

TRY YOUR VERY BEST TO
SHOW UP AND PARTICIPATE
IN FAMILY FUNCTIONS...
EVEN WHEN YOU REALLY
DON'T FEEL LIKE GOING.

!! NEWS FLASH !!

EVERYTHING ISN'T ABOUT WHAT
YOU WANT OR NEED.
SORRY 'BOUT THAT.

XO
DAD

6/31

JOB SECURITY

LEARN HOW TO SELL...
YOU'LL ALWAYS BE ABLE
TO FIND SUITABLE WORK.

XO

DAD

7/31

Greener Pastures

There's gonna be times when the grass looks so much greener on the other side of the fence. Sometimes, you'll just have to hop the fence and "Go for it".

XO
Dad

BTW... There's always gonna be more mowing & weeding than you planned for... So try not to "Burn Bridges".

8/31

THE TWIST

DANCE TO THE ORIGINAL
"TWIST" WITH YOUR
SIGNIFICANT OTHER AT
LEAST ONCE A MONTH.

XO
DAD

BTW... THROWING IN A FEW SLOW
DANCES ALONG THE WAY SURELY
CAN'T HURT THINGS ... EXCEPT
MAYBE SOME TOES.   ☺

9/31

POLITICS

REGISTER YOUR MIND AS
AN "INDEPENDENT" UNTIL
YOU'VE HAD A CHANCE TO
FACT CHECK THE CANDIDATES.
BE SURE TO VOTE!

XO
DAD

10/31

RELIGION

TOO MANY ORGANIZED RELIGIONS
CONTINUE TO EMBARRASS
AND GIVE GOD A BAD
REPUTATION ... DON'T BE
AFRAID TO SHOP AROUND.

X O

DAD

11/31

MONEY

THE LAST TIME I CHECKED,
IT'S NOT A CRIME TO BE
FINANCIALLY LITERATE AT A
YOUNG AGE.

XO
DAD

12/31

THE BIRDS & THE BEES

Go ask your mother.

X

Dad

13/31

COOKING

LEARN HOW TO BE HANDY
IN THE KITCHEN... YOU'LL
SAVE $$, EAT HEALTHIER AND
BE ABLE TO REASONABLY
PLAGARIZE CERTAIN DISHES
FROM YOUR FAVORITE
RESTAURANTS.

BON APPETIT

XO
DAD

14/31

BREAD & CHEESE

A HOUSE WITHOUT GOOD BREAD
AND CHEESE CAN NEVER
TRULY BE A HOME.

XO
DAD

15/31

WEAKNESS

EVERYBODY HAS A WEAKNESS
OR TWO THAT THEY WRESTLE
WITH ON A REGULAR BASIS ...
KEEP AN EYE ON YOURS IN
THE REAR VIEW MIRROR .

XO
DAD

16/31

TRASH TALK

ALWAYS AIM TO HAVE MORE
RECYCLING THAN TRASH.

XO
DAD

VOLUNTEER

Give a bit of your time and/or resources on a regular basis to a worthy cause in your community... You won't have to look very far.

XO
DAD

18/31

ANIMAL RESCUE

Do what you can.

xo
Dad

19/31

GRATITUDE THERAPY

AFTER YOU'VE TURNED OFF
THE LIGHTS AT THE END OF
A TROUBLESOME DAY, MAKE
A GRATITUDE LIST ... YOU'LL
BE SURPRISED AT HOW QUICKLY
YOUR WORRIES AND FEARS BEGIN
TO SOFTEN AND SHRINK.
NITE·NITE.

XO
DAD

LEAD, FOLLOW OR GET OUT
OF THE WAY.

— THOMAS PAINE

BTW... LEARN HOW TO DO ALL
THREE WELL.

XO
DAD

AFFECTION

Don't be too stingy
with hugs & kisses...
They are exfoliants
for our soul.

XOXOXOXOXOXO

Dad

ANGER MANAGEMENT

ANGER IS THE LOUDSPEAKER
FOR OUR FEARS...
LEARN TO RECOGNIZE AND MANAGE
YOUR FEARS — AND THEN YOU
WILL BE ABLE TO MANAGE YOUR
ANGER MUCH BETTER.
SPOILER ALERT! YOU'LL END UP
WITH LESS DAMAGE CONTROL IN
YOUR LIFE. ☺

BTW... IDENTIFYING AND ADMITTING
OUR FEARS CAN BE A LITTLE TRICKY.
SOME FEARS LIKE TO HIDE IN THE
NOOKS & CRANNIES OF OUR SUBCONSCIOUS.
JUST READ STEPHEN KING... HE KNOWS.

XO DAD

23/31

BRAKE PEDAL

LIFE HAS A NASTY LITTLE
HABIT, OF SUDDENLY CHANGING
DIRECTION WITHOUT ANY
WARNING...
NO TURN SIGNAL.
NO BRAKE LIGHTS.
NO FLASHERS.
AS YOU'RE CRUISING ALONG
THE ROAD OF LIFE MAKE A
HABIT OF PERIODICALLY TESTING
YOUR BRAKE PEDAL TO BE
SURE IT'S IN WORKING ORDER.
BEEP. BEEP.

XO
DAD

24/31

PLAN B

ALWAYS HAVE A WELL
THOUGHT OUT VIABLE PLAN B
IN YOUR BACK POCKET...
BECAUSE COMPOST HAPPENS.

XO

DAD

25/31

WISDOM

TO KNOW WHAT YOU KNOW
AND WHAT YOU DO NOT KNOW,
THAT IS TRUE KNOWLEDGE.

— CONFUCIUS

BTW... I THINK THE DUDE
WAS TELLING US TO GOOGLE
AND FACT CHECK MORE OFTEN.

XO
DAD

26/31

PICKING FLOWERS

DON'T PICK FLOWERS FROM
PUBLIC SPACES...
FIRST OF ALL, THEY'RE NOT
YOURS.
SECONDLY, THE REST OF US
BOZOS WONT BE ABLE TO
ENJOY THEM.

XO
DAD

Borrowing Stuff

Whenever you borrow stuff
do your very best to
return it on time.
Whenever possible, return
it in better shape
than when you borrowed it.

to

DAD

28/31

THANK YOU CARDS

THE LAST TIME I CHECKED,
HANDWRITTEN THANK YOU
CARDS ARE NOT ILLEGAL.

XO

DAD

29/31

OREO® COOKIE

BE CAREFUL ABOUT BOUNCING
AROUND TOO MUCH IN LIFE...
YOU'LL END UP KNOWING TOO
MUCH ABOUT BEGINNINGS AND
ENDINGS AND TOO LITTLE ABOUT
THE MIDDLE.
THE MIDDLE IS WHERE MOST
OF THE IMPORTANT STUFF IS...
KINDA LIKE AN OREO® COOKIE.

XO DAD

Raising Children

Raising children is kinda like tending to a flower garden...
Provide plenty of nourishment and sunshine.
Enjoy the blooms.
Weed when necessary.
Go easy on the compost.

XO
Dad

31/31

IT TAKES A VILLAGE...
— AFRICAN PROVERB

BUCKETS & BUCKETS OF KUDOS TO
TERESA MOORE AKA MAMA BEAR.
KUDOS ALSO TO THE MOORE-WISE
FAMILY AND THE WONDERFUL
CITY OF DES MOINES, IOWA.
THE GIRLS COULDN'T HAVE BEEN
RAISED BY A BETTER VILLAGE OR
IN A BETTER CITY.
THE GIRLS CONTINUE TO FLOURISH...

ACKNOWLEDGMENTS

Muchas Gracias to friends who have been the innocent victims of countless emails and texts during the lengthy development of this project. Thanks for the feedback. Thanks for the encouragement. Thanks for not blocking me.

Penny Brooks. Dave Mills.
Jim Newbury. Peter Guerin.
Shawn Nolan. Leighton.

Fred is retired and has finally returned to live in his beloved hometown of Burlington, Vermont.

This is his first book.

Printed in the USA
CPSIA information can be obtained
at www.ICGtesting.com
CBHW041346011124
16780CB00059B/1056